GOOD

ALWAYS

WINS

KIDS' EDITION

GOOD
ALWAYS
WINS
KIDS' EDITION

Written by ED STRAUSS

Illustrated by JUNE ARTHUR

BARBOUR BOOKS
An Imprint of Barbour Publishing, Inc.

© 2014 by Barbour Publishing, Inc.

Print ISBN 978-1-63058-384-2

eBook Editions:
Adobe Digital Edition (.epub) 978-1-63058-951-6
Kindle and MobiPocket Edition (.prc) 978-1-63058-952-3

Cover and interior illustrations by June Arthur.

Published by Barbour Books, an imprint of Barbour Publishing, Inc., P.O. Box 719, Uhrichsville, Ohio 44683 www.barbourbooks.com

Our mission is to publish and distribute inspirational products offering exceptional value and biblical encouragement to the masses.

 Member of the
Evangelical Christian
Publishers Association

Printed in the United States of America.
04834 1014 VP

CONTENTS

INTRODUCTION

The world around us can be very beautiful at times and can give us great happiness and joy, but it's also filled with pain, sadness, and injustice. Even if you are safe and happy, hundreds of millions of people around the globe are suffering in one way or another. Many are suffering greatly. This often causes adults and kids to wonder, *How could a God who loves us so much allow all this evil and misery?*

Millions of people in poor countries live in small tin shacks without electricity. They have very little food, no clean drinking water, no hope of an education, and no doctors. Some nations are at war with other nations, they fight civil wars, or terrorists attack them. And we don't have to look to foreign lands to see pain. People around us are suffering from diseases, traffic accidents, and other injuries. Some people are grieving because a family member has died. Others suffer when they're betrayed by a close friend—or bullied in school or on the Internet. If parents have divorced, this can cause kids grief. And some kids are sad because a parent has lost a job or their family has lost their home.

When these kinds of things happen, we often wonder, *Where is God? Why isn't He doing anything?* These are honest questions. We want to understand why God allows suffering. We wish to know that He actually cares. That is why this book was written—to answer these mysterious questions and to show that God loves us and has not abandoned us. He sees to it that good always wins.

1.

WHY DOES GOD ALLOW SUFFERING?

HABAKKUK ASKS GOD QUESTIONS

The Bible tells us that "God is love" (1 John 4:8 KJV). But there is sometimes so much pain around us that we wonder, *If God is love, why does He cause all this suffering? And if He doesn't cause it, why does He allow it? Since He's all-powerful, He could just stop it, couldn't He?*

Some people are afraid to question God. They think that shows that they don't trust Him. Or they worry that it makes Him angry. So they keep saying over and over, "God is good!" and never ask questions. It's true; God is good. He's very good. But that didn't stop the prophet Habakkuk from wondering why bad things happen.

Habakkuk trusted God so much that he said, "Even though the fig trees have no fruit and no grapes grow on the vines, even though the olive crop fails and the fields produce no grain, even though the sheep all die and the cattle stalls are empty, I will still be joyful and glad, because the LORD God is my savior" (Habakkuk 3:17–18 GNT). What trust! He was basically saying, "I don't care if absolutely *everything* goes wrong! Even if I have no food, I'm still going to be happy and love God!"

Yet Habakkuk wasn't afraid to ask God some very tough questions, such as, "How long, LORD, must I call for help, but you do not listen? Or cry out to you, 'Violence!' but you do not save? Why do you make me look at injustice? Why do you tolerate wrongdoing?" (Habakkuk 1:1–3 NIV). And guess what. God answered him!

So let's ask some honest questions about why God allows suffering and look at some of the answers.

. . . .

GOD LOVES AND CARES

God is all-powerful. The Bible tells us: "Behold, You have made the heavens and the earth by Your great power. . . . There is nothing too hard for You" (Jeremiah 32:17 NKJV). God created the entire universe! But some people think that after creating us, He left us to look after ourselves because He doesn't love us. Some think that He *would* care except that

He's just too busy. God is Lord of all creation, and He created some 170,000,000,000 (that's 170 billion!) galaxies in the universe, and each galaxy has millions or even trillions of stars. So yes, God is busy—very busy. He has the whole universe to look after, so why would He pay attention to our tiny planet, Earth?

Why? Because He's God. He's bigger than the whole universe.

God hasn't abandoned us or His creation. How do we know? The Psalms say, "The LORD is good to everyone. He showers compassion on *all* his creation" (Psalm 145:9 NLT, emphasis added). He loves us. He's our heavenly Father. Jesus said that God knows when even one sparrow falls to the ground—and we're worth more to Him than many sparrows (Matthew 10:29–31).

Our heavenly Father knows when even one sparrow falls to the ground—but still, the sparrow falls. Sometimes it might seem like God is not being good to everyone. So does God actually care? Yes. He cares. He feels our pain. The Bible reminds us, "The LORD is close to the brokenhearted" (Psalm 34:18 NIV). You may be too sad or worried to feel Him, but He's never far away when you're suffering. He's always very close.

GOOD, STEADY PHYSICAL LAWS

When God created the earth, He gave nature some rules for our good. For example, He created gravity to keep us from floating off into space. Gravity also keeps the earth's atmosphere from escaping. That's a good thing; otherwise we wouldn't have air to breathe. And because gravity works *all the time*, sparrows, and everything else, can fall. That's why you might break your leg if you fall off a rooftop.

Our heavenly Father made the moon to orbit around the earth, and this makes the tides rise and fall. God doesn't *have* to constantly do miracles to make the tides work. But He can do miracles. After all, He parted the Red Sea. He still does miracles today. But usually God lets things happen naturally.

They follow His laws of nature.

God created other laws as well, and they also work all the time. Jesus said that "he causes his sun to rise on the evil and the good, and sends rain on the righteous and the unrighteous" (Matthew 5:45 NIV).

So, if the sparrows still fall and people still suffer, how is God acting in love? Here's how: God will not stop working until He gets good out of any evil and suffering that happens. For sure, ever since Adam and Eve sinned and brought evil into the world, lots of bad things have happened. But God is able to bring good out of all bad situations in the end. "We know that all things work together for good to those who love God" (Romans 8:28 NKJV). God loves and cares for everyone all the time.

. . . .

PEOPLE MAKE SELFISH CHOICES

Some people agree that God is loving and that He cares a great deal about our suffering. But they also think that He isn't really all-powerful and that He can't answer all our prayers. Not true! The God who created the entire universe can do anything. But people ask, "If God does have the power to solve problems and stop suffering, why doesn't He?"

One of the main reasons is that, although God can do anything, He has limited Himself by giving us free will—the ability to choose what we will or will not do. The problem is that we often choose to do selfish, hurtful things—and choose not to do good. God doesn't usually stop us from making wrong choices. If He did, He'd be taking away our free will. Some people wish that He would. But then we'd all be mindless robots.

So because we have free will, our bad choices cause suffering in the world. This is why there is gossip, thefts, bullying, murders, and wars. But one day God will stop it! He says, "I, the LORD, will punish the world for its evil and the wicked for their sin" (Isaiah 13:11 NLT). The wicked cause great suffering, and God is not okay with that. The Bible tells us, "God is angry with the wicked every day" (Psalm 7:11 KJV).

Here is one example of selfish free will. Nearly 870 million people around the world go to bed hungry every night, and 15 million children die of starvation every year. What a terrible thing! But it doesn't need to happen. There's more than enough food to feed everyone! But wars stop farmers from harvesting food, and careless governments waste food. And people in wealthy nations throw away tons of food every day. Every year one-third of all food produced in the world—some 1.3 billion tons of it—is wasted instead of eaten! Selfish free will causes suffering.

YOU REAP WHAT YOU SOW

The Bible says, "A man reaps what he sows" (Galatians 6:7 NIV). If we're lazy and don't bother to brush our teeth, we get cavities. If we stuff ourselves with hamburgers just before going swimming, we get stomach cramps. If we're careless or in a panic, we can rush and cause accidents. This list goes on and on. Losing our tempers might make us say hurtful things and lose some friends. We might also lose our belongings if we don't look after them. It's easy to understand that we bring much suffering on ourselves. But the problem is that we expect God to, right away, fix all our messes, and we blame Him if He doesn't.

It's important to remember that we reap what we sow. If we set our minds on always trying our best to do what is right, then we might avoid some suffering. And when we mess up, if we honestly admit that we *caused* the problem and ask God to forgive us and help us *learn* from our mistakes, then we can spare ourselves some pain.

. . . .

PEOPLE DON'T PRAY

You might ask, "But what about accidents and diseases and robberies that aren't our fault? Why doesn't God stop those?" One reason is that God usually only does miracles when we pray. He doesn't normally stop the laws of nature or people's free will. However, He does promise to do something when we pray with all our hearts: "Call to me and I will answer you and tell you great and unsearchable things you do not know" (Jeremiah 33:3 NIV). And the apostle James reminds us, "You do not have because you do not ask" (James 4:2 NKJV). It sometimes takes real effort to pray, and many people don't want to put forth the effort.

And what about all those people who *do* pray, and God doesn't answer their prayers? We should remember the many times God *has* answered prayer and done miracles. Sometimes God is in the middle of answering prayer—and that can take time. When God doesn't answer right away, some people give up.

But here's what the Bible says: "Be patient in trouble, and *keep on* praying" (Romans 12:12 NLT, emphasis added). Although God is willing to act, some people don't have enough patience to wait. Or they lack faith that God is even listening. But God *is* listening, and we should never give up praying.

GOD JUDGES SIN

Sin can cause sicknesses or fears, or cause us to do things that hurt ourselves. Sin can also weaken our bodies, making it easier for diseases to attack. And yes, sometimes God judges sin by sending us a sickness that we wouldn't have gotten otherwise. When people in the Bible stubbornly disobeyed, the Lord sent troubles and sicknesses to punish them.

God also punishes Christians today. But our heavenly Father has a loving reason for this. He tells us, "Those whom I love I rebuke and discipline. So be earnest and repent" (Revelation 3:19 NIV). For sure this can be difficult. The author of the book of Hebrews says, "No discipline seems pleasant at the time, but painful. Later on, however, it produces a harvest of righteousness and peace" (Hebrews 12:11 NIV).

Some people forget that God *loves* us. All they can think about is that God is a holy God, that sin makes Him angry, and that He harshly judges sin. But is this really what God is like? Is every volcanic

eruption or earthquake or disease God judging a sinful world? Whenever anyone gets sick or is hurt, is God angrily punishing him or her for sinning? The answer is no. God is a loving God, and there are reasons other than sin that cause people to suffer.

THE DEVIL CAUSES SUFFERING

Some people believe that all disasters, diseases, problems, and accidents are caused by the devil and his demons. Everything bad that happens is "the works of the devil" (1 John 3:8 NKJV). While this isn't true in every case, it is true fairly often.

The Bible says, "The Son of God appeared. . . to destroy what the Devil had done" (1 John 3:8 GNT). Jesus is the Son of God and always good, and the devil is the worst bully and thief. He loves to rob people of health, peace, and happiness. This is why Jesus, filled with the Holy Spirit and with power, went about doing good and healing all who were oppressed by the devil (Acts 10:38). Jesus said, "The thief comes only to steal and kill and destroy; I have come that they may have life, and have it to the full" (John 10:10 NIV). Jesus came to rescue people from the devil's dirty tricks.

WHEN ANGELS DON'T PROTECT

The devil tries to attack us all the time, but God protects us. "His angel guards those who honor the LORD and rescues them from danger" (Psalm 34:7 GNT). When we love and trust God, the devil can't get past God's angels. God only allows him to cause us trouble if we have sinned—or if there is some very good reason. Job's life is a good example of this (see Job 1 – 2).

One day the angels of God came before the Lord, and Satan was among them. God knew that Satan wanted to bring grief to Job, so God asked him, "Have you noticed my servant Job? He is the finest man in all the earth."

Satan argued, "But reach out and take away his health, and he will surely curse you to your face!"

Then the Lord told Satan, "All right, do with him as you please. But spare his life." So Satan went out and struck Job with terrible boils from head to foot (Job 2:3 – 7 NLT).

Why did God allow the devil to cause such trouble to Job, a righteous man who had done nothing wrong? And why does God sometimes allow the devil to bring us grief as well? We'll look at this amazing answer in the next chapter.

So far, we've learned a few things about God: God is good all the time. He's very powerful, and even when it seems like He's far away, He's near to us. He gave nature good rules, and these rules always work. Because He loves us, God has given us free will, but we often choose bad things. The devil causes pain, but Jesus rescues us. God protects us when we pray, but He judges sin. The answers we've discovered prove that God is good, and good always wins!

2.

WHAT THE BIBLE SAYS ABOUT SUFFERING

THE BOOK OF JOB

The first Bible book that was ever written was Genesis. The book of Job was written next—even before Moses wrote the books of the Law. So Job is like a very old, very important key that opens up the rest of the Bible. If you want to understand why God allows suffering, you must read this book, because Job's story is all about suffering.

Here is a little history lesson that tells how people first learned about Job:

Job lived in the land of Uz, near the Dead Sea. In his day, the Israelites weren't living in Canaan. They were slaves in Egypt and were suffering greatly. "The Egyptians worked the people of Israel without mercy. They made their lives bitter, forcing them to mix mortar and make bricks and do all the work in the fields. They were ruthless in all their demands. . . . Years passed, and. . .the Israelites continued to groan under their burden of slavery" (Exodus 1:13–14; 2:23 NLT).

One day the Israelites' leader, Moses, killed

an Egyptian taskmaster. Then Moses ran away to Midian, next to the land of Uz, where Job had lived. Moses lived there for forty years. So how did the Israelites get a copy of the book of Job? Moses read it when he was in Midian. And when God finally sent Moses back to Egypt, he brought the book with him. Soon, all the Israelites knew about Job's suffering.

JOB'S FRIENDS ACCUSE HIM

Job was a very righteous man. He was also very rich and had a happy family. Then in *one day* he lost all his wealth and all his sons and daughters died. Job knew that these disasters didn't happen by chance. God Himself had allowed them (Job 1:13–21). Job had painful, disgusting sores for months (7:3–5). Day after day, all Job thought about was his suffering. But it made no sense. Like everyone else, Job believed that God always rewarded righteousness and judged sin. But he could think of nothing that he had done to deserve such punishment.

For years Job had been worrying. He knew that he was obedient, but Job also knew that sometimes bad things happened to good people. For example, plagues and diseases kill the innocent along with the guilty (9:22–24). Job had been worrying that although he was doing his best to live righteously, this might not keep all suffering away (3:25). And it didn't!

At first his friend Eliphaz told him to keep trusting God. Because he *was* righteous, God would soon bless him again (4:3–7). Another friend named Bildad agreed. "If you are pure. . .he will surely rise up and restore your happy home" (Job 8:6 NLT).

But a third friend, Zophar, thought that since no man was completely righteous, that Job must actually be guilty of secret sins. He suggested that God wasn't even judging Job as much as he deserved (11:6). So Zophar urged Job to repent and promised that if he did, God would take away all his troubles (11:13–20).

Job protested that he was innocent, but then all three friends began ganging up on him and insisting that he was suffering because he had sinned. And how did they *know* he had sinned? Because he was suffering! Finally, Eliphaz got so mad that, without any proof, he accused Job of doing absolutely terrible things (Job 22:5–11).

Job told them, "What miserable comforters you are!" He added, "If only you could be silent! That's the wisest thing you could do" (Job 16:2; 13:5 NLT).

. . . .

THE GOOD RESULTS OF SUFFERING

Everyone sins and God does judge sin, but that wasn't why Job suffered. Sometimes when *we* suffer, it isn't because God is judging us. Why would we have the book of Job in the Bible if it was only true for Job and no one else?

Why did God allow Job to suffer? Because God was working out His plan. The things Job suffered tested Job and made him a better person. Job recognized that God had a good reason for allowing all his troubles. He declared, "When He has tested me, I shall come forth as gold" (Job 23:10 NKJV). Isn't it great that God sees us as pure as gold?

And after Job suffered, God blessed him (see Job 42:10–17). The Bible says, "Brothers and sisters, as an example of patience in the face of suffering, take the prophets. . . . You have heard of Job's perseverance and have seen what the Lord finally brought about. The Lord is full of compassion and mercy" (James 5:10–11 NIV).

When we're suffering, it can be difficult to picture God as "full of compassion and mercy." But remember—it's not easy for God to see us suffer. Just like any good parent, it hurts Him. "He may bring us sorrow, but his love for us is sure and strong. He takes no pleasure in causing us grief or pain" (Lamentations 3:32–33 GNT).

. . . .

NAOMI'S SUFFERING

A woman named Naomi also suffered greatly. You can read her story in the book of Ruth. It goes like this:

There was a long famine in Israel, so Naomi, her

husband, and their two sons abandoned their farm in Bethlehem and went to a place called Moab to find food. After they'd lived there awhile, her sons married women from there. But just when it seemed that things were going well, Naomi's husband and both sons died.

Imagine how Naomi felt. First losing her house and her land. Then losing her husband and both sons. Now she would live in poverty. But what had she done wrong? The bad things that happened to her made no sense. Naomi told her daughters-in-law, "Things are far more bitter for me than for you, because the LORD himself has raised his fist against me" (Ruth 1:13 NLT).

Weeping, Naomi decided to return to her home. Her daughter-in-law Ruth went with her. And when Naomi returned to Bethlehem, her neighbors rejoiced to see her. They shouted, "Can this be Naomi?" Naomi answered, "Don't call me Naomi [which means Pleasant]. "Call me Mara [which means Bitter], because the Almighty has made my life very bitter" (Ruth 1:19–20 NIV).

But Naomi's story has a happy ending: Her daughter-in-law Ruth married a wealthy man in Bethlehem. She gave birth to a son who became an ancestor of David, Israel's most famous king. Naomi was once again happy and prosperous. Good won!

Did God let her suffer to punish her for sin? No. Naomi knew that she didn't deserve such punishment. That's why she was confused and depressed. She was like a female Job. Yet through her darkest days, God was working out His plan for her.

Job and Naomi were both discouraged because their suffering made no sense. Later on, however, they understood that God had tested them to purify them like gold. Someday, we, too, will understand the reasons for our suffering, when we meet God—but we may not understand before then.

WHY DO THE POOR SUFFER?

All trouble is *not* a result of God judging sin. If so, wicked people would be quickly punished. God would take away their riches just like He took away Job's. But sometimes wicked people seem to be blessed with wonderful lives. That's why Job asked, "Why do the wicked live and become old, yes, become mighty in power? . . . Their houses are safe from fear, neither is the rod of God upon them. . . . They spend their days in wealth" (Job 21:7, 9, 13 NKJV).

In the Law of Moses, God promised the Jews that if they sinned and disobeyed, He would judge them. But if they obeyed Him He would bless them. Despite these promises, however, God's people sometimes looked around and saw the wicked enjoying great wealth while sincere believers struggled with very little. Now, why was that?

When they prayed about it, they figured out that although it was normally good to have riches, and being wealthy was better than being poor, it was better to be poor and righteous than wicked and rich.

David said, "Better the little that the righteous have than the wealth of many wicked" (Psalm 37:16 NIV).

And Jesus said, "Blessed are you poor, for yours is the kingdom of God. Blessed are you who hunger now, for you shall be filled. Blessed are you who weep now, for you shall laugh. . . . But woe to you who are rich, for you have received your consolation. Woe to you who are full, for you shall hunger. Woe to you who laugh now, for you shall mourn and weep" (Luke 6:20–21, 24–25 NKJV). Those are powerful words from Jesus—and Jesus never lies.

LAZARUS AND THE RICH MAN

Jesus told this story: "There was once a rich man who dressed in the most expensive clothes and lived in great luxury every day. There was also a poor man named Lazarus, covered with sores, who used to be brought to the rich man's door, hoping to eat the bits of food that fell from the rich man's table. Even the dogs would come and lick his sores" (Luke 16:19–21 GNT).

Lazarus had no riches left and was covered with sores, just like Job. Lazarus sat on the ground suffering, just like Job.

But in Jesus' story, when Lazarus died he was carried by angels to be with Abraham in heaven. Abraham was the ancestor of all the Jews and was very close to God. The rich man also died but went to a bad place called Hades. "So he called out, 'Father Abraham! Take pity on me, and send Lazarus to dip his finger in some water and cool off my tongue, because I am in great pain in this fire!' But Abraham said, 'Remember, my son, that in your lifetime you were given all the good things, while Lazarus got all the bad things. But now he is enjoying himself here, while you are in pain'" (Luke 16:24–25 GNT).

You, too, may be receiving "bad things" right now. Like Job or Naomi or Lazarus, you may be suffering, and you may not be able to understand why. But know this: God sees your pain. He loves you. And one day you *shall* be comforted. And you *will* understand. The Bible says, "Now we see things imperfectly. . .but then we will see everything with perfect clarity" (1 Corinthians 13:12 NLT).

. . . .

HAVE COMPASSION ON THE SUFFERING

The Bible doesn't always explain why God allows people to suffer, but it does show us how we should act toward those who are in pain.

Job's friends said that he had sinned and brought all this trouble on himself. But Job replied, "I have heard many things like these. . . . I also could speak like you, if you were in my place; I could make fine speeches against you and shake my head at you. But my mouth would encourage you; comfort from my lips would bring you relief" (Job 16:2, 4–5 NIV).

And that's exactly what Jesus did. He went everywhere encouraging, comforting, and bringing relief to people. "When he saw the crowds, he had compassion on them, because they were harassed and helpless, like sheep without a shepherd" (Matthew

9:36 NIV). Jesus said, "The LORD has anointed Me. . .he has sent Me to heal the brokenhearted. . .to comfort all who mourn" (Isaiah 61:1–2 NKJV). And guess what! We are to do the same.

Paul tells us, "Weep with them that weep" (Romans 12:15 KJV). But it's hard to weep with others if we suspect that God is punishing them for sinning. Then we think, *Hmmm. . .God is angry with them. So I won't be kind to them either. I'll just stand back and let God punish them.*

When trouble comes to people around us, it's tempting to think that they must have sinned. In some cases this may be true. We don't know. But, remember: when God allows others to suffer, He's also closely watching *our* hearts—whether we'll sit back and judge or reach out with mercy. Instead of trying to guess someone's secret sins, we should pray for them, comfort them, and help them. When we do that, good wins!

Brothers and sisters, as an example of patience
in the face of suffering, take the prophets. . . .
You have heard of Job's perseverance and
have seen what the Lord finally brought about.
The Lord is full of compassion and mercy.
JAMES 5:10–11 NIV

3.

WHY DISEASE AND DISABILITIES?

THE MAN BORN BLIND

It was the devil who caused Job to suffer from painful sores. So we know that the devil and his demons can bring disease. When healing people, Jesus sometimes cast out an evil spirit that was causing the sickness. However, most of the time when someone was sick, Jesus simply healed them. What does this mean? It means that most sick people do *not* have evil spirits dwelling inside them. The spirits just attacked them and made them sick.

Some people say that God wouldn't have allowed the devil to give someone a disease or some handicap unless they had sinned. Even Jesus' disciples believed it. "Now as Jesus passed by, He saw a man who was blind from birth. And His disciples asked Him, saying, 'Rabbi, who sinned, this man or his parents, that he was born blind?'" (John 9:1–2 NKJV).

Back then, many rabbis—religious teachers—argued that all disease was punishment for sin. They thought that if a baby was born with a handicap that either (a) God had judged the baby to punish his *parents* for sinning, or (b) *the baby* had sinned while in the mother's womb. Think about it. How could a baby sin before even being born?

What did Jesus say? He answered His disciples, "Neither this man nor his parents sinned, but that the works of God should be revealed in him" (John 9:2–3 NKJV). Jesus then healed the man, and this good "work of God" (healing) caused many people to believe in Him (John 10:41–42).

- -

WHY GOD ALLOWS SICKNESSES

The "works of God" are not just healing—although it's wonderful when they are! We feel miserable when we're sick, but sometimes God uses sickness to do a good work in our lives. One believer told God, "Before I was afflicted I went astray, but now I keep Your word" (Psalm 119:67 NKJV). He added, "My suffering was good for me, for it taught me to pay attention to your decrees" (Psalm 119:71 NLT). Suffering also causes us to pray and get close to God.

God knows that suffering is painful, but He also knows that good can come from it. He tells us, "I have refined you, but not as silver is refined. Rather, I have refined you in the furnace of suffering" (Isaiah 48:10 NLT). In biblical times, when silver was melted in a furnace, the junk mixed in with it *also* melted. Then the junk floated to the surface and was scooped off. When we're in a furnace of suffering, it can purify us. Suffering can accomplish good. It can make us into better people.

The Bible says, "Trouble produces endurance" (Romans 5:3 GNT), and Joseph is a good example of this. After his brothers had sold him as a slave into Egypt, he told them, "You meant evil against me; but God meant it for good. . .to save many people alive" (Genesis 50:20 NKJV). However, it took *years* for God to work out His plan. Joseph had to spend thirteen years in slavery and in prison before God brought great good out of his suffering. In the meantime, he suffered injustice, shame, and pain. But good won in the end.

DOES GOD ALWAYS HEAL?

What about healing for our bodies in this life? Many Bible verses tell us that God can do miracles to heal people. Much of Jesus' time was spent healing people—and the apostle James told us exactly how to pray for healing (see James 5:14–15). So we should definitely pray for people who are sick. But we can't insist that it's God's will to heal *everyone*.

Paul had a great healing gift and did amazing miracles. But even he couldn't heal a faithful friend. Instead, he wrote, "Trophimus have I left at Miletum sick" (2 Timothy 4:20 KJV). Have you ever experienced this? Have you ever missed a special event or had to stay behind because you were sick? The same thing happened to Paul's friend, Trophimus.

Another one of Paul's friends named Timothy "was sick so often" in his stomach. When Paul couldn't heal him, he simply gave him health advice and told him how to take care of himself (1 Timothy 5:23 GNT). And Paul himself had a disease that he couldn't get rid of, although he prayed three times (2 Corinthians 12:7).

Remember, God can heal and does heal. But He's not like a genie in a bottle. He doesn't do miracles every time we command.

. . . .

WHY DID GOD CREATE BACTERIA?

We know that germs (bacteria and viruses) are responsible for many illnesses. So the question is, why did God create them?

Bacteria can cause diseases from sore throats to leprosy to the bubonic plague. The bubonic plague killed 100 million people in Europe and Asia from 1338 to 1351. No wonder many people think that *all* bacteria are bad!

But most are harmless, and many do tremendous good. Billions and billions of good bacteria live in the human body—about five hundred different species of them, in fact. Many of them produce vitamins we need or help us to digest food. We couldn't survive without them. They're part of God's "very good" creation.

Then why do some bacteria cause disease and death? It wasn't this way when the world was first created when "God saw everything that He had made, and indeed it was very good" (Genesis 1:31 NKJV). However, we live in a damaged world. Mankind's disobedience brought a curse on the earth (Genesis 3:17–18; Isaiah 24:5–6), and this was when some bacteria changed and became harmful.

WHY DID GOD CREATE VIRUSES?

Viruses cause sicknesses such as influenza, hepatitis C, dengue fever, and HIV (which may turn into AIDS). Viruses are such simple things that they can't even reproduce. They have to invade other cells (bacteria or plants or humans), take them over and make them produce more viruses.

Since they cause much evil and almost zero good, they weren't part of God's original creation. They probably were formed when Adam and Eve sinned, changing from bacteria or plasmids (pieces of DNA that move between cells) into viruses. Even evolutionary scientists believe that there was a change that created viruses, though they don't believe that God created the world—or that the world is suffering because of Adam and Eve's sin.

But God told Adam, "The ground is cursed because of you" (Genesis 3:17 NLT). Paul added that "all creation was subjected to God's curse," and that one day, when the kingdom of God is established, "the creation looks forward to. . .freedom from death and decay" (Romans 8:20–21 NLT). When that happens, there will be no more viruses.

· ·

WHAT CAN WE DO?

Until the day that God makes the world new, there are things Christians can do to help others.

Some 200 million people in tropical countries have malaria, a disease that mosquitoes carry. Malaria kills over 700,000 people every year. Yet malaria can be cured. There are good medicines for it. But often poor people can't afford the medicines. Good wins when we give money to help fight diseases in poor countries.

Cholera is a serious sickness caused by unclean water and sewage that gets into food. Nearly 5 million people in poor countries get sick from cholera every year, and some 120,000 die. This is why Christian aid workers dig deep wells for poor villages. This is why doctors and nurses travel around teaching villagers how to keep their places clean. Good wins when we help by donating even a little money to their work. Good also wins when we donate our time to helping those in need.

Good wins when we care for the elderly who are sick. Good wins when believers encourage a special needs child to be all that she can be. Good wins when Christians act like Jesus and show God's love and compassion to anyone in need.

God's love caused a Samaritan to stop on the Jericho road to help an injured man (Luke 10:25–37). And Jesus said, "Truly I tell you, whatever you did for one of the least of these brothers and sisters of mine, you did for me" (Matthew 25:40 NIV). Love is God's answer to help those suffering in the world. Think of some things you can do to show God's love right in your own neighborhood.

. . . .

GOD WILL RESTORE US ONE DAY

The Bible promises Christians that one day "God will wipe away every tear from their eyes; there shall be no more death, nor sorrow, nor crying. There shall be no more pain" (Revelation 21:4 NKJV). What a wonderful promise! So remember that this life is not the end. There is heaven afterward, and "this small and temporary trouble we suffer will bring us a tremendous and eternal glory" (2 Corinthians 4:17 GNT).

Our physical bodies may be weak now. They may suffer from disease. We may have serious physical challenges. We may have to stay in a wheelchair, or even a bed. But one day our bodies will be changed into powerful, eternal bodies. "Our bodies are buried in brokenness, but they will be raised in glory. They are buried in weakness, but they will be raised in strength. They are buried as natural human bodies, but they will be raised as spiritual bodies" (1 Corinthians 15:43–44 NLT).

Yes, this life is often unfair. Things aren't always made right in this world. All sick people aren't made well—though many *can* be. But all sicknesses and handicaps will be made right in the bright world that's coming. This hope has been a great comfort to millions of people down through the ages. And knowing that someday we will live in a perfect world is very good!

This small and temporary trouble we suffer
will bring us a tremendous and eternal glory.
2 Corinthians 4:17 GNT

4.

WHY NATURAL DISASTERS?

ARE DISASTERS "ACTS OF GOD"?

When earthquakes, volcanoes, and tsunamis cause disasters, lawyers call them "acts of God." This simply means that these disasters aren't caused by humans. But many people literally think that these *are* special acts of God. They think that these aren't natural disasters at all, but that every time one happens, God is personally causing it to happen.

Why do they believe this? Well, they think that since God is all-powerful and rules the nations, He must *also* personally cause all disasters, great and small. But what could His reasons be for causing such disasters?

If an earthquake strikes China, some people insist that God judged China because many of its people don't believe in Him. If an earthquake strikes Greece, they argue that God judged them because they're not *true* Christians. If an earthquake strikes California, they say that God judged them for turning from the truth. But if an earthquake strikes their *own* neighborhood, they don't know what to think. Perhaps their *neighbors* sinned?

The fact is, millions of earthquakes happen all the time—only most of them are far too small to cause any damage or even be noticed. They're so microscopic that they can only be picked up by delicate instruments. Surely God doesn't spend His time, day in and day out, causing teeny quakes. So is there another explanation? There is.

WHY EARTHQUAKES HAPPEN

Science tells us that the earth's outer crust is broken up into seven or eight large sections called *plates*. These plates are slowly moving. As the ocean floor spreads apart, they push the plates. Large heat currents in the earth's mantle also push the plates along. If two plates hit each other, mountain ranges like the Himalayas get pushed upward. If one plate slides under another, volcanoes create mountains; the Andes Mountains are examples of this.

The enormous pressures from these bumping plates escape in bursts of energy called earthquakes.

If earthquakes happen at sea, they can cause giant tidal waves called tsunamis.

Another thing: most of Earth's volcanoes sit on the edges of the Pacific plate and on the edges of the other huge plates. Hot magma rises up between the cracks in the plates. This is what causes many volcanoes.

God told the Israelites to settle in Canaan right beside the Arabian plate, and that's why they experienced lots of earthquakes. Some of these were huge and destructive. Others were just big enough to draw people's attention to important events—such as the earthquake that happened when Jesus died and the earthquake that shook the ground when He resurrected (Matthew 27:50–54; 28:1–2).

So we see that God is perfectly able to *make* earthquakes happen. But normally these disasters are caused by the natural laws He already set in place. And just like His law of gravity, God allows the moving plates to keep moving along. He doesn't constantly do miracles to stop them.

BUT CAN'T GOD PROTECT US?

You might ask, "Even if God doesn't *cause* every single earthquake, can't He do miracles to protect people from them?" Yes, He can. And sometimes He does. People have miraculously survived terrible earthquakes. You might also wonder, *Can't God warn people to flee to a safer place?* Again, the answer is yes. God sometimes has people leave a building just before a quake makes it collapse. He doesn't do this every time, but He *does* do it at times. Often God commands us not to enter dangerous situations in the first place. For example, if you build your house on a

rumbling volcano, you know you're setting yourself up for trouble.

The Bible promises that God will protect those who love and obey Him. "The Lord says,

'I will rescue those who love me. I will protect those who trust in my name. When they call on me, I will answer; I will be with them in trouble'" (Psalm 91:14–15 NLT). This is a good promise to remember, especially if you live in a place that has lots of earthquakes!

But just because you're a Christian doesn't mean that God will *always* protect you from *every* danger or trouble. He often does, and you can be very thankful for that. But sometimes, for reasons we don't understand, Christians suffer in disasters along with other people. We can't always understand why this happens, but one day we'll see God face-to-face, and we'll understand.

DROUGHTS AND FAMINES

Droughts and famines also cause people to question God.

In the Old Testament, God sometimes kept it from raining. He warned, "If a country sins and is unfaithful to me, I will reach out and destroy its supply of food. I will send a famine" (Ezekiel 14:13 GNT).

But the Lord also promised that He would *stop* a famine if His people repented. "When I shut up heaven and there is no rain. . .if My people who are called by My name will humble themselves, and pray and seek My face, and turn from their wicked ways, then I will hear from heaven, and will forgive their sin and heal their land" (2 Chronicles 7:13–14 NKJV). This is where people get the idea that all droughts and famines are caused by sin.

When God made the world to be inhabited, He created it with rich soil and rainfall. Paul said, "The living God, who made the heavens and the earth. . .has shown kindness by giving you rain from heaven and crops in their seasons; he provides you with plenty of food and fills your hearts with joy" (Acts 14:15–17 NIV). God still sets up the weather to bring blessings, but the curse stops it from being perfect.

God doesn't make the weather perfect. He hasn't promised to constantly watch over the weather of every country. He only promised to be personally involved with the weather of one country all year long—the land of Israel (see Deuteronomy 11:11–12).

NATURAL REASONS FOR WEATHER

Some of worst droughts are mentioned in the Bible, and God doesn't say that He sent them as judgments. God just let them happen. In Abraham's day, there was a long drought in Canaan. It caused a famine and Abraham was forced to go to Egypt for a while (Genesis 12:10). Some years later, his son Isaac was forced to move because of another drought (Genesis 26:1). The fact is, every so often the weather gets really, really dry in that part of the world.

Different parts of the world have their own wild weather. Typhoons often cause great damage in the Philippines and China, not because the people sin, but because that's just what the weather is like there. For the same reason we get hurricanes on the East Coast and tornadoes from Texas to Kansas. It rains throughout the year in Seattle, but it's bone dry in Death Valley. Weather is different in different places.

You might think that God personally decides every single time it should rain or not rain, but He has set up His natural laws and the weather follows these laws. God sometimes does step in and change the weather when we pray. But no matter how much you pray, you probably aren't going to get tropical heat at the South Pole in the middle of winter.

MAN IS WRECKING THIS WORLD

It's not "acts of God" that cause most suffering, but mankind's own ignorance and selfishness. Genesis 2:15 (NIV) says, "The LORD God took the man and put him in the Garden of Eden to work it and take care of it." God wants people to care for this world, but we're now reaping the results of *not* caring for it. "For they have sown the wind, and they shall reap the whirlwind" (Hosea 8:7 KJV).

For example, chopping down all the trees and unwise ways of farming cause the land to lose its soil and become deserts. Dry countries, like Spain and Greece, were once covered with forests and received more rainfall. Their weather became dry when their forests disappeared. Sometimes selfish industries pollute our soil, water, and air. They empty poisonous waste into our streams, our lakes, and our oceans. Pollution makes the air too smoggy to breathe in some cities.

It's clear that much of humanity's suffering is our own fault. Ever since Adam and Eve's disobedience in the Garden of Eden, people have been destroying themselves and their world.

ACTS OF LOVE AND MERCY

Good wins when God's children react to disasters with love and mercy.

In Bible times, the Christians in Antioch heard that a great famine was coming and would hit Judea very hard. Instead of sitting around wondering who had sinned to cause the famine, they took action. "The disciples decided that they each would send as much as they could to help their fellow believers who lived in Judea" (Acts 11:29 GNT).

God also wants us to do what we can to feed the

hungry, clothe the poor, and help disaster victims. Read Matthew 25:31–46 and you'll see what it means to be a follower of Jesus Christ. Read the story of the good Samaritan in Luke 10:25–37 and you'll understand God's love for the world. He wants *us* to help those who are suffering. "Dear children, let us not love with words or speech but with actions and in truth" (1 John 3:18 NIV).

This is why Christians have always been leaders in doing acts of mercy and compassion. They supply food during famines, build orphanages and hospitals, and run homeless shelters and soup kitchens. And Christians give generously to help destroyed areas rebuild after earthquakes and tsunamis. These are the *true* "acts of God."

"When I shut up heaven and there is no rain
. . .if My people who are called by My name
will humble themselves, and pray and seek
My face, and turn from their wicked ways,
then I will hear from heaven, and will
forgive their sin and heal their land."
2 Chronicles 7:13–14 NKJV

5.

WHY WARS AND SENSELESS VIOLENCE?

MAN'S HATRED CAUSES WARS

Love should be the foundation of all our relationships. Jesus said, "'You shall love the LORD your God with all your heart, with all your soul, and with all your mind.' This is the first and great commandment. And the second is like it: 'You shall love your neighbor as yourself'" (Matthew 22:37–39 NKJV).

Some people think that loving others is a nice idea *if* they can manage it. But their love wears thin quickly with difficult people. And when it comes to loving their *enemies?* Forget it! They want nothing to do with them. Yet Jesus said that if we are His followers we must not only love our friends and neighbors, but even those who hate us (Matthew 5:44–45).

When He told the story of the good Samaritan, He was teaching that we must love other human beings, no matter what their race, nationality, or religion. If we do, we'll respect them and avoid doing things to hurt them. "Love does no wrong to others" (Romans 13:10 NLT). Love does good things to others. But when we have prejudice and hatred, all kinds of negative things happen.

The Bible asks, "From whence come wars and fightings among you? Come they not. . .of your lusts?" (James 4:1 KJV). Often nations fight because one nation lusts for another nation's land, oil, or water, and tries to take it. Or sometimes they lust for revenge because of something the other nation did in the past.

God told the Israelites, "I command you today to love the LORD your God. . .and to keep His commandments" (Deuteronomy 30:16 NKJV). And one of His most important commandments is, "You shall love your neighbor as yourself" (Leviticus 19:18 NKJV). When we do that, then good wins!

WHY DOESN'T GOD STOP HATRED?

God gave us clear commands, and still, people continue hating and hurting others. So you might ask, "Why doesn't God just stop them if they won't obey?"But if God were to always step in and prevent *all* crimes before they even happened, He'd have to stop every selfish, wrong thing that any of us do. This is simply not going to happen.

God will one day judge everyone and reward them or punish them for what they've done. But for now, He's left justice up to us. He's told us clearly in the Bible that we are to set up strong laws to protect the weak, discourage criminals, and hand out justice. Over and over again, the Bible commands God's people to care for the weak and helpless people. "Pure and genuine religion in the sight of God the Father means caring for orphans and widows in their distress" (James 1:27 NLT). If a nation's people don't do this, God warns that He will judge that country.

· ·

DEFENDING YOUR COUNTRY

War causes much suffering. That's why some people think nations shouldn't fight at all, not even to defend themselves when armies attack them. While most wars are caused by selfishness and hate, there *are* righteous wars. God expects the military to protect its nation from evil. He expects the police to arrest criminals (see Romans 13:1–5). Jesus said, "When a strong man, fully armed, guards his own house, his possessions are safe" (Luke 11:21 NIV).

Our men and women in uniform work hard to protect us. Sometimes they even sacrifice their lives. War can be very violent, and at times good people die along with the bad. When soldiers or police officers suffer an injury or die, we should remember and honor them for it. Jesus said, "Greater love has no one than this, than to lay down one's life for his friends" (John 15:13 NKJV).

THE WAR ON TERROR

The Battle of Britain in 1940 was a terrible time. London was mercilessly bombed over and over while British warplanes fought life-or-death battles with German warplanes and bombers in the dark skies above. It was an awful period in Britain's history. It was a time of great suffering and anxiety. Yet it is also remembered as their "Finest Hour" because they fought so bravely and refused to give up.

Today many countries are fighting a war on terror. This battle is happening in America and all around the world, and it won't be won easily.

America's war on terror began when terrorists crashed passenger jets into the Twin Towers in New York on September 11, 2001. This caused great destruction, and many innocent people lost their lives. When the dust settled, Americans realized that they were at war. They knew that the terrorists wanted to make them afraid, but for most people it had the opposite effect: it made them rise up and refuse to be pushed around. It also brought Americans together as a nation and stirred them to action. Terrorist attacks can cause fear and destruction, but they can also bring out the best and most heroic side of people.

TERRIBLE ATTACKS CREATE HEROES

In recent years, violent people have brought pain and suffering in America—when the Murrah Building was bombed in Oklahoma; when a gunman shot moviegoers in a theater in Aurora, Colorado; when innocent people were killed and injured by a bomb during the Boston Marathon—in each case, Americans saw how cruel human beings can be.

In the middle of these dark moments, however,

acts of heroism shine brightly. We will never forget the 343 firefighters who rushed up the steps of the burning Twin Towers to rescue others, and lost their lives as a result. And right after the Boston bombings, many people ran *toward* the explosions to help others. They didn't even consider their personal safety. And think of the brave people who lost their lives while protecting a loved one in the Aurora movie theater.

Such terrible attacks often move people to loving actions. When they hear what has happened, they do something to show that they care. For example, someone starts a website for the people who have been hurt, and donations pour in. When people are shocked by evil, it encourages them to know that there's also a great amount of good in this world as well.

Kind people doing good deeds can't bring our loved ones back. It can't make all the pain go away. But when we need to know that their lives meant something, when we need to know that others share our grief, these loving actions mean a lot. We may not understand why God allows bad things to happen, but we know that He cares because *others* care.

· ·

WHAT CAUSES VIOLENT ACTS?

God has given us free will, but some people choose to do evil, so there has been violence in the world since the beginning. Don't forget that Adam and Eve's son, Cain, killed his brother Abel (Genesis 4:8). And in Noah's day, thousands of years ago, the world was so full of violence that God finally had to step in and destroy it (Genesis 6:10–13).

In the last days of the earth, things will get very violent again. The Bible warns, "But know this, that in the last days perilous times will come: For men will be. . .without self-control, brutal, despisers of good" (2 Timothy 3:1–3 NKJV). "But evil men. . .will grow worse and worse" (2 Timothy 3:13 NKJV). Finally, Jesus will return to judge the world again.

We can't blame God for what people do. After all, they're doing the exact opposite of what He said. They're breaking His command to love their fellow man. So we understand that one day He will judge them. But it can be hard to wait for that day.

When we hear of fires at gas wells, explosions at fertilizer plants, speeding trains going off the rails, and buses driving off the highway, it's clear that *people* are at fault. People were careless or made a mistake. God didn't cause it. In fact, God often brings details to our attention to prevent accidents

Accidents happen, and often they cause grief. If someone's parent was injured in an accident at their job, or they died in a traffic collision, their families feel great loss. They can't help but ask, "Why did God let them get hurt or die?"

. . . .

DEALING WITH GRIEF

There are often no easy answers to "Why, God?" questions. And since there are different answers for each situation, it's not wise to give everyone the same answer.

When someone is grieving the loss of a loved one, it's not usually a good idea to try to guess why God allowed them to die. We just can't know God's reasons. Simply being there and sharing their sorrow is more important than trying to explain it.

Job's friends made a mess when they tried to guess what had caused Job's troubles. But they had the right attitude at first. When they heard about his troubles they went to visit him. "When they saw him. . .they began to weep aloud. . . . Then they sat on the ground with him for seven days and seven nights. No one said a word to him, because they saw how great his suffering was" (Job 2:12–13 NIV).

One of the dangers in trying to explain disaster is that people often say things like, "Well, I guess God needed another angel in heaven," or "Don't be sad. He's with God now." The grieving person has every right to be sad. So allow them to grieve. . .and grieve *with* them.

"'You shall love the LORD your God with all your heart, with all your soul, and with all your mind.' This is the first and great commandment. And the second is like it: 'You shall love your neighbor as yourself.'"
MATTHEW 22:37–39 NKJV

6.

MONEY AND RELATIONSHIP PROBLEMS

TITHING AND GOD'S BLESSING

Many Christians believe that if they tithe (give 10 percent of their money to their church), that God will then pour out His blessings on them. He will bless them with all the money they need, keep them in good health, solve all family problems, prevent accidents, and keep away trouble. They also believe that if Christians don't tithe, God will curse them by sending them money problems, sickness, family arguments, accidents, and many other problems. They get this idea from these verses: "Should people cheat God? Yet you have cheated me! But you ask, 'What do you mean? When did we ever cheat you?' You have cheated me of the tithes and offerings due to me. You are under a curse, for your whole nation has been cheating me. Bring all the tithes into the storehouse. . . . If you do," says the LORD of Heaven's Armies, "I will open the windows of heaven for you. I will pour out a blessing so great you won't have enough room to take it in! Try it! Put me to the test!" (Malachi 3:8–10 NLT).

Those are powerful promises, and many Christians who have faithfully given 10 percent of their income to God have been blessed mightily—not just with material things, but in other ways. And most of all, they're blessed spiritually because, as Jesus said, "It is more blessed to give than to receive" (Acts 20:35 KJV).

* *

BLESSED FOR GIVING GENEROUSLY

The Jews who lived in Old Testament times were commanded to tithe. But many Christians don't think that this law applies to believers today. That's because in the New Testament, Jesus and the apostles said almost nothing about tithing. However, they said a great deal about giving money generously.

Jesus promised, "Give, and you will receive. Your gift will return to you in full—pressed down, shaken together to make room for more, running over, and poured into your lap. The amount you give will determine the amount you get back" (Luke 6:38 NLT).

Paul encouraged Christians to give by saying, "Remember that the person who plants few seeds will have a small crop; the one who plants many seeds will have a large crop" (2 Corinthians 9:6 GNT). The idea is clear: God will bless you a little if you give little, and bless you a lot if you give generously.

Jesus didn't promise that what we "get back" would be all money or other material things. God gives us many kinds of blessings. But the good news is that finances are part of these blessings, since God has promised to supply everything we need (Philippians 4:19). And millions of people have discovered that as they tithe or give to others, God does bless them. They might not have great riches, but they have enough—and for this they are grateful.

. . . .

WHY WE SOMETIMES LACK

Some Christians have found out that although they tithe faithfully to their church and give to the needy, the blessings they hoped to receive aren't poured out on them. They still have to get by with little cash, the same old clothes, no new video games, sickness, family problems, and other troubles.

Why is this? The simple answer is that God is not a bubble-gum machine where we put in our money, turn the handle, and out come the goodies. He is Almighty God. Yes, He has promised to supply everything we need (Philippians 4:19), but many things we think we need are not actually *needs*. They're just things we *want*.

But what if our family is so short on cash that there's not enough money to pay all the bills? Sometimes we lack because God *is* withholding His blessings to get our attention. He isn't cursing us. But He *is* disciplining us. "Those whom I love I rebuke and discipline. So be earnest and repent" (Revelation 3:19 NIV).

Sin can block God's blessing from coming to us. The Bible says, "Your iniquities have turned these things away, and your sins have withheld good from you"

(Jeremiah 5:25 NKJV). So if something in our lives *is* displeasing God, we should ask Him to point it out so that we can ask His forgiveness and change our ways.

. . . .

LIFE ISN'T ALWAYS EASY

There are other reasons why we lack. If we're poor, it doesn't mean that we're not giving or that we're sinning somehow. (Remember Job and Lazarus!) The surest sign that God is blessing us isn't that we have money and material things. It's that we have God's Holy Spirit and His love and His joy in our hearts, and that we have godly character.

And how do we *get* godly character? Usually it's formed when we go through hardships and problems. Hard tests and troubles make our virtues grow. This can be difficult to accept if our goal is only to have lots of nice things, the newest toys, and nothing but pleasure.

There's nothing wrong with having nice things

as long as we don't forget that "we *must* go through *many* hardships to enter the kingdom of God" (Acts 14:22 NIV, emphasis added). And hardships mean suffering. Millions of Christians in poor nations earn barely enough money to get by. They hardly ever treat themselves. And many Christians in America are in the same situation.

Sometimes Christians suffer because they *are* Christians. Paul warned that "everyone who wants to live a godly life in Christ Jesus will suffer persecution" (2 Timothy 3:12 NLT). Believers in many countries are often persecuted and "share abundantly in the sufferings of Christ" (2 Corinthians 1:5 NIV). They're not allowed to have well-paying jobs and they're often treated badly. Do they have lots of new clothes, yummy snacks, and electronic toys? No. They feel blessed if they have a roof over their heads, enough food to eat, and clothing to wear.

Does God *really*, honestly expect us to be content if we lack? Yes. The apostle Paul wrote, "I have learned to be content whatever the circumstances. I know what it is to be in need, and I know what it is to have plenty. I have learned the secret of being content in any and every situation, whether well

fed or hungry, whether living in plenty or in want"
(Philippians 4:11–12 NIV).

. . . .

BEING HAPPY IN TOUGH TIMES

Often Paul didn't have much money. But he did have
lots of troubles. He said, "We are pressed on every side
by troubles, but we are not crushed. We are perplexed,
but not driven to despair" (2 Corinthians 4:8 NLT).
(To be perplexed is to wonder *what on earth* God is
doing in our lives.) We, too, are sometimes pressed by
troubles and often perplexed. Being perplexed and
pressed down with trouble causes us to suffer.

Jesus tells us not to despair or become
discouraged no matter what happens. He said, "In
this world you will have trouble. But take heart! I have
overcome the world" (John 16:33 NIV). So let's trust
God. We can do this even in bad situations.

Paul wrote about the Christians of northern
Greece, "They are being tested by many troubles,
and they are very poor. But they are also filled with

abundant joy" (2 Corinthians 8:2 NLT).

God wants us to be happy and to have peace—and not just when everything is going our way. Paul tells us, "Always be full of joy in the Lord. I say it again—rejoice!" (Philippians 4:4 NLT).

· ·

PAIN IN RELATIONSHIPS

Relationships between parents and children, between brothers and sisters, and between friends bring us some of our happiest moments. But sad to say, they can also sometimes bring us great stress and grief. Many of us know what it's like to be judged unfairly. We know what it's like to be betrayed by a person we loved and trusted. We know what it's like to have someone tell us that they're not our friend anymore. This can really hurt.

It's bad enough to deal with the pain of being rejected. But when the problem really begins is when we want to hurt people back, when we want to make them feel pain, too. Being filled with bitterness and a desire for revenge not only wrecks our relationship with people but also our relationship with God.

The Bible says, "Do not seek revenge or bear a grudge against anyone among your people, but love your neighbor as yourself" (Leviticus 19:18 NIV). When we have a grudge against someone or seek revenge on them, we're not loving them—and when we don't love them, we don't love God. "Whoever claims to love God yet hates a brother or sister is a liar. For whoever does not love their brother and sister, whom they have seen, cannot love God, whom they have not seen" (1 John 4:20–21 NIV).

The key to good relationships is to love and to *keep* on loving. "Love is patient, love is kind. . . . It does not dishonor others, it is not self-seeking, it is not easily angered, it keeps no record of wrongs" (1 Corinthians 13:4–6 NIV). How do we keep from holding a grudge against someone? By not keeping a list of wrongs and by continually forgiving them. That doesn't mean we should try to be best friends with someone who doesn't want to be friends anymore. But we can at least be kind to that person.

Jesus commanded us to love even our *enemies* (Matthew 5:44–45). This means loving people who are no longer friends. It also means loving family members even when they bug us. When we replace hatred and anger with love, good wins.

*Whoever claims to love God yet hates
a brother or sister is a liar. For whoever
does not love their brother and sister,
whom they have seen, cannot love God,
whom they have not seen.*
1 JOHN 4:20-21 NIV

7.

DOES GOD TRULY CARE?

WHEN GOD DOESN'T ANSWER PRAYER

Sometimes we might feel that there's no good explanation for suffering. Any person, good or bad, can end up suffering. There's some truth to this. The Bible tells us, "People are born for trouble as readily as sparks fly up from a fire" (Job 5:7 NLT). That's the way life is. We all get sick. We all feel pain. We all have accidents.

Yes, our own suffering helps us offer sympathy to others who suffer. Yes, we've been surprised by bad situations that turned out very good (Romans 8:28). But if we've suffered for a long time, while bad people have no trouble at all, we may feel this way: "There is something else meaningless that occurs on earth: the righteous who get what the wicked deserve, and the wicked who get what the righteous deserve" (Ecclesiastes 8:14 NIV).

Even with trying to do what's right, we're not always blessed with wealth, health, or good friends. God does reward righteousness, and He *does* answer prayer, but not always the way we expect. And sometimes we might think that He's not answering our prayers at all.

. . . .

IS GOD DISTANT FROM OUR TROUBLES?

At times we may feel like Job. His friends tried to encourage him that if he'd just hang in there, sooner or later God would bless him again. But like Job, some of us may wonder if this will ever happen. We're sometimes like Naomi: we think that God Himself has made up His mind to cause us grief, so it's difficult to believe that He will ever bless us again.

People tell us that "God is love" and that He loves us personally. But we can sometimes be so confused by what God allows to happen that we may think He actually doesn't care. Sometimes it can appear like God isn't there for us.

We usually can't notice God with our physical senses. And since we can't see Him, it's easy to get the idea that He's not around. And when it seems that our prayers aren't being answered, we might ask, like King David, "Why do You stand afar off, O LORD?

Why do You hide in times of trouble?" (Psalm 10:1 NKJV). This not only confuses us but can give us the feeling that life just doesn't make sense.

. . . .

WHEN LIFE DOESN'T MAKE SENSE

Much suffering in life seems to be senseless, and if this life is all there is, then many things truly *would* be senseless.

Consider how unfair this story would be if death is the end. You've read it before, but read it again: "There was a certain rich man who was splendidly clothed in purple and fine linen and who lived each day in luxury. At his gate lay a poor man named Lazarus who was covered with sores. As Lazarus lay there longing for scraps from the rich man's table, the dogs would come and lick his open sores. Finally, the poor man died. . . . The rich man also died" (Luke 16:19–22 NLT).

What if that's where the story ended? One man lives with great wealth, perfect health, and no troubles. Yet right next to him, another man (who didn't do anything wrong) lives in great poverty, daily hunger and sickness, and no end of misery—then they both die. What would we think of the love of God if that was the end of the story?

But the story doesn't end there. The death of our physical body isn't the end. Jesus went on to say that Lazarus "was carried by the angels to be with Abraham" (22). And Abraham explained to the man who had once been rich, "Son, remember that during your lifetime you had everything you wanted, and Lazarus had nothing. So now he is here being comforted" (Luke 16:25 NLT).

The Bible explains exactly how people like Lazarus are comforted in heaven. "They are before the throne of God, and serve Him day and night in His temple. And He who sits on the throne will dwell among them. They shall neither hunger anymore nor thirst anymore; the sun shall not strike them, nor any heat;

for the Lamb [Jesus] who is in the midst of the throne will shepherd them and lead them to living fountains of waters" (Revelation 7:15–17 NKJV).

Death of our bodies does not mean the end. Christians can look forward to life forever in heaven. For those who believe in Jesus, good always wins.

. . . .

THINGS ARE MADE RIGHT IN HEAVEN

Jesus said, "In My Father's house are many mansions; if it were not so, I would have told you. I go to prepare a place for you" (John 14:2 NKJV). And Paul reminds us, "No eye has seen, no ear has heard, and no mind has imagined what God has prepared for those who love him" (1 Corinthians 2:9 NLT).

Heaven is more wonderful than we can imagine. "God will wipe away every tear from their eyes; there shall be no more death, nor sorrow, nor crying. There shall be no more pain. Then He who sat on the throne said, 'Behold, I make all things new'" (Revelation 21:4–5 NKJV). Our brief life on earth may be filled with sorrow and injustice, but this world we live in now only lasts a short while. The wonderful life in heaven will last forever.

The promise of eternal life and never-ending joy seems almost too good to be true. How can we be sure that such a paradise really exists? Because Jesus said, "If it were not so, I would have told you" (John 14:2 NKJV). And Jesus always tells the truth. That's how we know.

. . . .

JESUS' SUFFERINGS

So how do we get to heaven? Jesus explained, "I am the way and the truth and the life. No one comes to the Father except through me" (John 14:6 NIV). God sent His Son to earth to become a man, to experience all the pain and sorrow that we experience, and to die on the cross for our sins. "For God so loved the world that he gave his one and only Son, that whoever believes in him shall not perish but have eternal life" (John 3:16 NIV).

Job, Naomi, and Lazarus all suffered, but Jesus was the ultimate example of a righteous man who was rejected, falsely accused, and suffered a shameful death. And the cross was just *part* of His suffering. The Bible tells us, "Then Pilate took Jesus and had him flogged" (John 19:1 NIV).

This was a brutal torture. Jesus was first stripped naked and His hands were tied to a whipping post. Then two Roman soldiers, one standing behind to the left, the other to the right, began beating Him. They whipped His shoulders, His back, His buttocks, and His upper legs—all the way down to His feet.

The Roman whip was called a *flagellum*. It had a wooden handle with strips of leather. Many lead balls and pieces of bone were tied to each strip. At first they broke open the blood vessels below the skin. Then the blows cut through the skin. As the beating went on and on, they slashed Jesus' muscles. Jesus' back was soon cut wide open. The pain was absolutely terrible, and He lost much blood. This left Jesus so weak that He was unable to carry His cross (Luke 23:26).

JESUS' CRUCIFIXION

Crucifixion was the worst torture and death. Its goal was not just to kill its victims, but to kill them in the most painful way possible. Iron nails were driven between Jesus' wrist bones, cutting through a major nerve as they pinned His hands to the cross. The pain was intense. After that, they pounded a nail through His feet.

Jesus could breathe in while hanging down, but to breathe out He had to raise Himself up. To do that, He had to push upward against the nail in His feet and pull against the nails in His wrists. This caused unbelievable

pain. His back, cut open by the flogging, scraped against the rough wood of the cross as He pulled Himself up then slumped down again and again.

When Jesus was nailed to the cross, "The soldiers gave him wine mixed with bitter gall" (Matthew 27:34 NLT). These words in the Bible explain how Jesus felt: "Their insults have broken my heart, and I am in despair. If only one person would show some pity; if only one would turn and comfort me. But instead, they give me poison [gall] for food; they offer me sour wine for my thirst" (Psalm 69:20–21 NLT).

Like Job, Jesus felt punished and abandoned by God. With His final breath He called out, "My God, My God, why have You forsaken Me?" (Matthew 27:46 NKJV). Jesus actually felt that His Father had abandoned Him. Being rejected by His people was bad enough. But feeling rejected by God was more than He could bear. Some medical doctors believe that Jesus actually died of a broken heart.

THE GREATEST INJUSTICE

Remember that verse: "There is something else meaningless that occurs on earth: the righteous who get what the wicked deserve, and the wicked who get what the righteous deserve" (Ecclesiastes 8:14 NIV).

Jesus did not deserve to suffer. And to those who loved Jesus—when God seemed to be standing back doing nothing—this was the greatest injustice.

But this story has the happiest of all possible endings. After lying dead in a tomb for three days, Jesus was raised from the dead, by God, with great power. His disciples saw Him alive again after His crucifixion. He now lives forever and reigns at the right hand of His Father in heaven. And by His suffering and His dying, He paid the price for all of our sins and made a way for *us* to enter heaven. Jesus' death on the cross made it possible for death to be defeated, all injustices to be corrected, and all suffering to be made right.

By His crucifixion and His resurrection, Jesus brought wonderful meaning to a world filled with pain and suffering. And there is more wonderful news for us. Jesus said, "Because I live, you will live also" (John 14:19 NKJV).

When Jesus came back to life after He died, good won! And it won forever.

GOD MAKES ALL THINGS RIGHT

This world is eventually going to come to an end, and Jesus will reign over all the nations. The entire world will be turned into a paradise like the Garden of Eden. Then heaven will come down to the earth, and God will dwell among us.

When our loved ones die, it leaves a huge empty space in our hearts. But we will once again be united with them, and we'll be with them on the heavenly new earth forever. In that day, all our tears will be dried, and all of our questions will be answered.

In the meantime, people will always suffer. Paul said that he welcomed suffering for Jesus' sake because he wanted to "know Him and the power of His resurrection, and the fellowship of His sufferings" (Philippians 3:10 NKJV). But the good news is this: "If we suffer, we shall also reign with him" (2 Timothy 2:12 KJV). Can you imagine ruling over the earth with Jesus?

God sees all of our pain. And although He doesn't step in to prevent every accident, sickness, or disaster, He loves us and cares immensely. When God saw the suffering of the Hebrews in Egypt, He said, "I know their sorrows" (Exodus 3:7 NKJV). He knows every bit of our sorrows too. He knows every tear that we cry. He knows when we have grief. He personally feels our pain. "In all their suffering he also suffered" (Isaiah 63:9 NLT). It hurts God to see us suffer.

God doesn't cause evil, but in His great love for us, He constantly turns evil situations into good ones. He won't stop until good comes out of every bad situation. God is good. He is loving. As David said, "You *are* good, and *do* good" (Psalm 119:68 NKJV, emphasis added).

There is suffering in the world. But the good news is this: one day all our suffering will come to an end, and we will enjoy happiness and great joy in heaven forever.

Now you know. Good always wins!

God will wipe away every tear from their eyes;
there shall be no more death, nor sorrow,
nor crying. There shall be no more pain.
Then He who sat on the throne said,
"Behold, I make all things new."
REVELATION 21:4–5 NKJV

BIBLE
PROMISES
TO
REMEMBER

GOD COMFORTS ME

Christ encourages you, and his love comforts you. God's Spirit unites you, and you are concerned for others.

PHILIPPIANS 2:1 CEV

Even though I walk through the darkest valley, I will fear no evil, for you are with me; your rod and your staff, they comfort me.

PSALM 23:4 NIV

Remember your promise to me; it is my only hope. Your promise revives me; it comforts me in all my troubles.

PSALM 119:49–50 NLT

May our Lord Jesus Christ himself and God our Father encourage you and strengthen you in every good thing you do and say. God loved us, and through his grace he gave us a good hope and encouragement that continues forever.

2 THESSALONIANS 2:16–17 NCV

Nevertheless God, who comforts the downcast, comforted us.

2 CORINTHIANS 7:6 NKJV

Show me a sign for good, that those who hate me may see it and be ashamed, Because You, LORD, have helped me and comforted me.

PSALM 86:17 NKJV

Heavens and earth, be happy. Mountains, shout with joy, because the LORD comforts his people and will have pity on those who suffer.

ISAIAH 49:13 NCV

I find true comfort, LORD, because your laws have stood the test of time.

PSALM 119:52 CEV

GOD GIVES ME COURAGE

Wait on the LORD: be of good courage, and he shall strengthen thine heart: wait, I say, on the LORD.

PSALM 27:14 KJV

God did not give us a spirit that makes us afraid but a spirit of power and love and self-control.

2 TIMOTHY 1:7 NCV

Above all else, you must live in a way that brings honor to the good news about Christ. Then, whether I visit you or not, I will hear that all of you think alike. I will know that you are working together and that you are struggling side by side to get others to believe the good news. Be brave when you face your enemies. Your courage will show them that they are going to be destroyed, and it will show you that you will be saved.

PHILIPPIANS 1:27–28 CEV

And now, dear children, remain in fellowship with Christ so that when he returns, you will be full of courage and not shrink back from him in shame.

1 JOHN 2:28 NLT

Wait for the LORD's help. Be strong and brave, and wait for the LORD's help.

PSALM 27:14 NCV

When I asked for your help, you answered my prayer and gave me courage.

PSALM 138:3 CEV

GOD GIVES ME EVERYTHING I NEED

The lions may grow weak and hungry, but those who seek the LORD lack no good thing.

PSALM 34:10 NIV

And my God shall supply all your need according to His riches in glory by Christ Jesus.

PHILIPPIANS 4:19 NKJV

He gives food to those who fear him; he always remembers his covenant.

PSALM 111:5 NLT

As for the rich in this world, charge them not to be proud and arrogant and contemptuous of others, nor to set their hopes on uncertain riches, but on God, Who richly and ceaselessly provides us with everything for [our] enjoyment.

1 TIMOTHY 6:17 AMP

Once I was young, and now I am old. Yet I have never seen the godly abandoned or their children begging for bread.

PSALM 37:25 NLT

May he give you what you want and make all your plans succeed.

PSALM 20:4 NCV

"Acknowledge the God of your father, and serve him with wholehearted devotion and with a willing mind, for the LORD searches every heart and understands every desire and every thought. If you seek him, he will be found by you."

1 CHRONICLES 28:9 NIV

GOD GIVES ME HOPE

For I know the thoughts that I think toward you, says the LORD, thoughts of peace and not of evil, to give you a future and a hope.

JEREMIAH 29:11 NKJV

Since we have such [glorious] hope (such joyful and confident expectation), we speak very freely and openly and fearlessly.

2 CORINTHIANS 3:12 AMP

You are my refuge and my shield; your word is my source of hope.

PSALM 119:114 NLT

But the LORD looks after those who fear him, those who put their hope in his love.

PSALM 33:18 NCV

My soul faints for Your salvation, but I hope in Your word.

PSALM 119:81 NKJV

Moreover [let us also be full of joy now!] let us exult and triumph in our troubles and rejoice in our sufferings, knowing that pressure and affliction and hardship produce patient and unswerving endurance. And endurance (fortitude) develops maturity of character (approved faith and tried integrity). And character [of this sort] produces [the habit of] joyful and confident hope of eternal salvation. Such hope never disappoints or deludes or shames us, for God's love has been poured out in our hearts through the Holy Spirit Who has been given to us.

ROMANS 5:3–5 AMP

GOD GIVES ME JOY

Shout to the LORD, all the earth. Serve the LORD with joy; come before him with singing.

PSALM 100:1–2 NCV

"I am coming to you now, but I say these things while I am still in the world, so that they may have the full measure of my joy within them."

JOHN 17:13 NIV

Not that we have dominion [over you] and lord it over your faith, but [rather that we work with you as] fellow laborers [to promote] your joy, for in [your] faith (in your strong and welcome conviction or belief that Jesus is the Messiah, through Whom we obtain eternal salvation in the kingdom of God) you stand firm.

2 CORINTHIANS 1:24 AMP

Is anyone amoung you in trouble? Let them pray. Is anyone happy? Let them sing songs of praise.

JAMES 5:13 NIV

For our heart shall rejoice in Him, because we have trusted in His holy name.

PSALM 33:21 NKJV

Singing psalms and hymns and spiritual songs among yourselves, and making music to the Lord in your hearts.

EPHESIANS 5:19 NLT

So now we can rejoice in our wonderful new relationship with God because our Lord Jesus Christ has made us friends of God.

ROMANS 5:11 NLT

GOD GIVES ME STRENGTH

I know how to live when I am poor, and I know how to live when I have plenty. I have learned the secret of being happy at any time in everything that happens, when I have enough to eat and when I go hungry, when I have more than I need and when I do not have enough. I can do all things through Christ, because he gives me strength.

PHILIPPIANS 4:12–13 NCV

My body and mind may fail, but you are my strength and my choice forever.

PSALM 73:26 CEV

"The righteous keep moving forward, and those with clean hands become stronger and stronger."

JOB 17:9 NLT

God is awesome in his sanctuary. The God of Israel gives power and strength to his people. Praise be to God!

PSALM 68:35 NLT

That you may walk worthy of the Lord, fully pleasing
Him, being fruitful in every good work and
increasing in the knowledge of God; strengthened
with all might, according to His glorious power,
for all patience and longsuffering with joy;

COLOSSIANS 1:10-11 NKJV

The LORD gives strength to his people; the LORD blesses
his people with peace.

PSALM 29:11 NIV

GOD HAS A PLAN FOR ME

"For I know the plans I have for you," declares the
LORD, "plans to prosper you and not to harm you,
plans to give you hope and a future."

JEREMIAH 29:11 NIV

But God led his people out like sheep and he guided
them like a flock through the desert. He led them to
safety so they had nothing to fear.

PSALM 78:52-53 NCV

Lean on, trust in, and be confident in the Lord with all your heart and mind and do not rely on your own insight or understanding. In all your ways know, recognize, and acknowledge Him, and He will direct and make straight and plain your paths.

PROVERBS 3:5-6 AMP

"If this is true, let me know what your plans are, then I can obey and continue to please you. And don't forget that you have chosen this nation to be your own." The LORD said, "I will go with you and give you peace."
EXODUS 33:13-14 CEV

The LORD is my shepherd, I lack nothing. He makes me lie down in green pastures, he leads me beside quiet waters, he refreshes my soul. He guides me along the right paths for his name's sake.
PSALM 23:1-3 NIV

GOD HEARS ME

"In that day you will not ask me for anything. I tell you the truth, my Father will give you anything you ask for in my name. Until now you have not asked for anything in my name. Ask and you will receive, so that your joy will be the fullest possible joy."

JOHN 16:23–24 NCV

"Here's what I want you to do: Find a quiet, secluded place so you won't be tempted to role-play before God. Just be there as simply and honestly as you can manage. The focus will shift from you to God, and you will begin to sense his grace. The world is full of so-called prayer warriors who are prayer-ignorant. They're full of formulas and programs and advice, peddling techniques for getting what you want from God. Don't fall for that nonsense. This is your Father you are dealing with, and he knows better than you what you need. With a God like this loving you, you can pray very simply."

MATTHEW 6:6–11 MSG

As bad as you are, you still know how to give good gifts to your children. But your heavenly Father is even more ready to give good things to people who ask.

MATTHEW 7:11 CEV

GOD IS ALWAYS WITH ME

Is there anyplace I can go to avoid your Spirit? to be out of your sight? If I climb to the sky, you're there! If I go underground, you're there! If I flew on morning's wings to the far western horizon, You'd find me in a minute—you're already there waiting! Then I said to myself, "Oh, he even sees me in the dark! At night I'm immersed in the light!" It's a fact: darkness isn't dark to you; night and day, darkness and light, they're all the same to you.

PSALM 139:7–10 MSG

My old self has been crucified with Christ. It is no longer I who live, but Christ lives in me. So I live in this earthly body by trusting in the Son of God, who loved me and gave himself for me.

GALATIANS 2:20 NLT

Know, recognize, and understand therefore this day
and turn your [mind and] heart to it that the Lord is
God in the heavens above and upon the earth
beneath; there is no other.

Deuteronomy 4:39 amp

"But will God really dwell on earth? The heavens,
even the highest heaven, cannot contain you.
How much less this temple I have built!"

1 Kings 8:27 niv